VIETNAM VIGNETTES

VIETNAM VIGNETTES

War As Seen Through The Eyes of a Non-Combatant

JOHN PHILIP LIBERTO

XULON PRESS

Xulon Press
2301 Lucien Way #415
Maitland, FL 32751
407.339.4217
www.xulonpress.com

Paperback ISBN-13: 978-1-66287-087-3
Ebook ISBN-13: 978-1-66287-088-0

DEDICATION

I dedicate this booklet to my grandkids:
Jenson Butler, Jennings Butler, Carter Liberto, and
Ellen Liberto.

ACKNOWLEDGMENTS

I COULD NOT HAVE WRITTEN THIS BOOK without the support and inspiration from my wife, Sandra. Also, I want to thank Betty Disher for the many hours she spent editing my story and correcting my sentence structure and punctuation.

TABLE OF VIGNETTES

INTRODUCTION

IT HAS NOW BEEN MORE THAN FIFTY-FOUR years since I was discharged from the Army. Veteran's Day always seems to bring back some memories of the two years that I served in the Army and especially the twelve months I served in Vietnam. I realized, like most others, that the older I get the less I can remember, so I decided on Veterans' Day of 2020 to begin writing down the memories of my time in the service before they are mostly gone.

I don't have a combat story to tell because I was not in the infantry. I was drafted into the Army five days before I was to register for college. After boot camp, where I was taught discipline, taught to be a team player, and taught how to fight, the Army eventually trained me to be a helicopter mechanic, not a warrior, but I do have a story to tell. It's not one continuous story; instead, it's a series of small stories or vignettes. Hence, the title of this booklet.

VIGNETTE ONE
BOOT CAMP

ON THE MORNING OF FEBRUARY 16, 1966, my father dropped me off at the Selective Service Center in Memphis where about twenty of us young men, both black and white, were about to become members of the military. We had been drafted.

We lined up in our civilian clothes, were told to raise our right hands, and then were sworn in by an Army officer. The Marines were three men short of their monthly goal of recruits and we were asked for three volunteers to join the Marines instead of the Army. Nobody volunteered, so the Marine recruiter walked down the line and picked out three men and told them they were now Marines. Those poor souls left with the recruiter while the rest of us boarded a bus for the Memphis airport. There we boarded a civilian DC-3 where I was seated by the window overlooking the right wing. This would be my first trip in an airplane. Soon we were on our way to Fort Polk, Louisiana, which is near Shreveport, for eight weeks of basic training, also called "boot camp."

As soon as we arrived at basic training, we were bombarded with drill instructors yelling in our faces. They didn't want a conversation with us. All they wanted was for us to yell back saying, "Yes, sir!", and then to do what they said to do. We got all of our hair shaved off. Then stripping down to our underwear, we walked single file between a line of doctors and nurses who were giving us shots in both arms at the same time. We were then measured and given our uniforms.

Over the next eight weeks, we slowly became soldiers. We learned how to march together, how to fight hand to hand, how to stab the enemy with a bayonet, how to shoot Vietnamese fighters with a M-14 rifle, and how to take our rifles apart and clean them. Most important of all, we learned to work as a team under extreme conditions and to obey orders without hesitation. We also had classes on the Unified Code of Military Justice where we learned what we could do and what not to do in a war.

The last week before graduation we had to run the confidence courses. One day, we ran nine miles with all of our heavy equipment on our backs and our rifles in our hands. I completed it, but some did not. That night, we had to crawl under barbed wire in the mud for fifty yards with our rifles while live machine gunfire whizzed over our heads. We also had to crawl around exploding pits to reach the end. Again, I completed it, so I was able to graduate and go home for a couple weeks.

All of us soldiers from Memphis boarded a train in Shreveport and headed back to our hometown. The train ride was uneventful until we arrived in Jackson, Mississippi where the train stopped for an hour or so. Several of us decided to find a restaurant to get a bite to eat since there was no food on board. That turned out to be a big mistake. We thought nothing about the few Blacks being in our group. We had all been through boot camp together and had become friends. We were just hungry soldiers looking for a meal. As soon as we entered the crowded restaurant, the room got quiet as everyone turned and stared at us. We were soon surrounded by Jackson police officers. The manager then notified us that they didn't serve Blacks there and suggested that there would be no "sit in" at his restaurant.

We were all in US Army uniforms. We had all just finished basic training, and we all would be entering the Vietnam War within a few weeks. But in Mississippi we were not welcome because there were a few Blacks with us. This was at the height of "sit in" demonstrations in the South, but none of us were thinking about that. We were just hungry. We immediately left before there was any trouble and headed back to the train.

Early the next morning, we arrived back in Memphis. After a two-week leave with family, I flew to Ft. Carson, Colorado for helicopter repair technical training. Two months of training passed and the Army thought that I was ready for the "big time," so after another short leave with family, I was on my way to Vietnam. I was only nineteen years old, but I had become a man in just a few months

VIGNETTE TWO

WELCOME TO VIETNAM

I ARRIVED AT SAIGON'S TAN SON NHAT International Airport aboard a Braniff 707 with a couple hundred other soldiers in July of 1966. We were all wearing our short sleeve dress summer khaki uniforms. None of us had more than one stripe on our sleeves. We had taken off from Oakland making refueling stops in Hawaii, Tokyo, Guam, and the Philippines before landing in Saigon about twenty hours later. I had only been in the army six months, but the Army said that we were ready for the big time.

The mood as we prepared to land was somber. Some of us were reading the small New Testament Bibles all of us were issued. Others were praying or holding crucifixes. A few were quietly crying, and some were just staring out the windows. The vast majority of us were about nineteen or twenty years old. As each one of us departed the plane, the stewardesses told us that they would see us again in one year and take us all back home. At the time I didn't know if I believed them or not.

4

We were bused to "Tent City" about ten miles from the airport to be processed into the country which would take a couple of days. The bus ride through the crowded streets of Saigon was like nothing I had ever experienced before. There appeared to be no traffic rules. Every driver and pedestrian was on his own. Tent City was actually a little city composed of dozens of large olive-drab army tents. Not only did it house hundreds of soldiers, but there were mess halls to feed us, laundries for our uniforms, latrines and showers, a post office, and a post exchange, also known as PX. The PX was similar to a Walmart, so I went there soon after arriving where I bought some stationery and envelopes to write home. The stationery had a Vietnam letterhead with a dragon at the top. The envelopes had the same dragon off to the left side. I wrote a few letters to family and friends that first day even though I didn't have much to tell them. No stamp was required; instead, we just wrote "free" on the top right corner. We were encouraged to write home often.

After a couple of days, a sergeant came into my tent and called out twenty or twenty-five names. Mine was one of them. I thought he told us we were leaving by train at 2200 hours, or 10:00 p.m. That concerned me because traveling by train in a war zone didn't seem very smart or safe to me. A few others heard the same thing. We learned later that what he said was that we were all going to Nha Trang by bus, not by train. That was a relief to me.

A bus picked us up at 10:00 p.m. promptly and drove us to a waiting camouflaged C-130 transport plane. The engines were running and lights were flashing on its wings and tail. The rear ramp was down, and we filed in with all of our equipment except our weapons. They would be issued later when we got to our posts. We sat in red strap seats with our backs along each sidewall of the plane. There were no windows. The sound inside was deafening. All we could do was sit there and stare ahead. After a few more minutes, we were off into the wild black yonder. It took an hour or so for our plane to arrive over Nha Trang. Little did we know that soon all hell would break loose. We were about to be introduced to the Vietnam War in a big way, but none of us were prepared for what would happen next.

VIGNETTE THREE
THE REALITY OF WAR

I COULD TELL THE PLANE WAS CIRCLING and was about to land. Then the sergeant began walking up and down in front of us, yelling to be heard over the roaring of the engines. He said that the base at Nha Trang was under attack, and the plane would not be coming to a complete stop. After landing, it would taxi and then immediately take off again to protect itself from gunfire. It was a big target. Our only job was to get off the plane while it was taxiing so it could quickly take off again.

We felt the bump as the wheels hit the ground. The plane slowed down quite a bit, but it kept moving. Soon, the rear ramp dropped, but didn't hit the pavement. The order was given, and we began running down the ramp. I followed the guy in front of me who followed the guy in front of him and so on. I took a running jump off the end of the ramp which was about eighteen to twenty-four inches above the tarmac. As soon as my boots hit the ground, I realized that I had just landed in another world.

It was mass confusion! Using today's terminology, it was as if I was suddenly inside a video game over which I had no control; like someone was working the controls, and I was just reacting – running as fast as I could. Parachute flares were illuminating the midnight sky. We heard continuous gunfire. There were explosions and fires. A small spotter plane circled overhead. Gunships were emptying their Gatling guns of red tip tracer bullets into the surrounding mountains.

We did not stop. My leg muscles were burning as the strap of my duffle bag was digging into my right shoulder, but I kept running as did everyone else. We must have run for two or three hundred yards down the tarmac. We finally came to the end of the runway where a barbed wire fence kept us from going any farther. There were some sandbag bunkers there, and we all jumped in for protection so that we could catch our breaths. It was a miracle that none of us had gotten hurt. I crouched down in a corner and began praying for my own safety. I confessed repeatedly all of the sins that I had committed in my entire nineteen years that I could remember. I also made promises to God that, sadly, I would later break.

After a few hours, the video game ended. The flares went out, the gunfire stopped, the fires had been put out, and it got very dark and quiet. The sky was clear, and the stars were bright. We were all safe, but nobody knew what to do next. The sergeant had stayed on the plane, and it appeared that we were on our own. Nobody could sleep, and we all discussed what we had gone through in just a few short hours. I realized then that it was a good thing that we didn't have our weapons yet. We could have done serious damage to the wrong people including ourselves in the confusion. I remember watching the sun begin to rise over the mountains in the distance and wondering how something could be so beautiful in such a hellish place.

We saw a truck heading our way shortly after the sun was up. It was a "Deuce and a Half" troop hauler, a two-and-a-half-ton truck. A sergeant got out and asked what we were doing there. We told him that we got off a plane running, and this is where we ended up. Then he asked who was in charge. When someone answered, "Nobody," his face turned red and he let loose a barrage of four-letter words. He reminded us that we were soldiers and that somebody always, *always* had to be in charge! If it ever appeared that nobody was in charge, it was our duty to take charge – a great life lesson.

We had all failed our first wartime test. We climbed into the back of the truck with our duffle bags, and he dropped us off at our company headquarters. I can honestly say that night was the most terrifying night of my life up to that time.

VIGNETTE FOUR
LIEUTENANT FUZZ

THE 339TH TRANSPORTATION COMPANY headquarters was a rectangular concrete block building painted a faded lime green and had a corrugated metal roof. There were several windows on each side which were screened, but not glazed for air circulation purposes. Each window had a metal shutter that was hinged from the top which could be lowered to keep the sun and rain out. There was a thermometer on the right side of the door which read ninety degrees. Later in the day, it would read 120 degrees.

From the front door out to about twenty-five feet was a perforated steel walkway about six feet wide. A flagpole about fifteen feet tall was on the right-hand side near the end of the walkway where the American flag and the company flag fluttered. Around the pole was an approximately ten-foot diameter circle of faded white painted stones. On the left side was a matching faded-white painted stone circle with a bulletin board full of informational sheets near its center. There was little to no landscaping around the building – no grass, just dirt, sand, and a few scraggly plants.

We were greeted by a very young-looking second lieutenant who welcomed us to the 339th. I forgot his real name, but everyone called him "Lieutenant Fuzz" because he looked just like the lieutenant in the *Beetle Bailey* cartoon. He took himself very seriously. He pointed in the direction where we could find the mess hall and the PX before taking us to our barracks which had a similar shape and construction as the headquarters building. We picked out our bunks, which had mosquito nettings, and we dropped off our duffle bags. There were no footlockers at the end of the bunks; instead, there were large wooden wardrobes for each of us for our clothing and personal items. Down the center aisle were the gun racks.

Next, he marched us to the quartermaster building where we picked up our bedding and helmets. The last stop was the armory where we were finally issued weapons and ammunition. He let us know that it would be a few days before most of us would begin working our assigned jobs at the airfield because our slots weren't open yet. That meant the soldiers we were replacing had a few more days left before rotating back to the States. He said that we would be on detail duty until then and that he was the detail officer. Early the next morning after breakfast, we fell in for inspection from Lieutenant Fuzz. He said he had a job for us that would last all day – filling sandbags and building a new bunker behind the mess hall. He left us alone without another word.

It was another very hot day, and it was miserable work. We removed our shirts, but I was still sweating like crazy and got filthy from the mixture of sweat and sand. There were about ten of us. Someone eventually took charge and suggested that we take turns filling the bags and placing the bags on the bunker walls. That gave us a little change of motion every hour or two. We worked all day in the heat, stopping only for water breaks and lunch. We built a nice secure bunker about eight feet high with a twenty-four inch wide opening at one end. One soldier began complaining that he didn't come to Vietnam to fill sandbags in 120 degree heat. Another reminded him that he could have been out in the jungle with the infantry where unseen people would be shooting at him in the 120 degree heat. That stopped his complaining.

I was surprised at how many Vietnamese, both men and women, were working on the base, and they seemed to have free access to every building. The mess hall was staffed with Vietnamese. There was a young girl called Boop who would keep our barracks clean. She was always dressed the same: black pajama bottoms, a white blouse, and a bamboo conical hat. She cleaned the mud off our boots and took our dirty clothes to the laundry for us. She swept the floor with the typical Vietnamese short straw broom which caused her to bend over while sweeping just like every other woman in the country. Whenever she sat down, she would squat on the floor rather than use a chair. It cost each of us about two dollars a month for the service, and she was glad to get that.

VIGNETTE FIVE
WORK DETAILS

WE WERE INSPECTED BY LIEUTENANT Fuzz the next morning after breakfast in the common area outside of our barracks again. After inspection, he told us to meet him at the motor pool in an hour. He said that we were to wear our helmets and bring our weapons and ammunition belts. We talked among ourselves as we checked our equipment, wondering what Lieutenant Fuzz was about to get us into. This was the first time I'd been in battle gear with live ammo since boot camp back in Fort Polk, Louisiana. We were all a little nervous to say the least. We were sent to Vietnam as aircraft repairmen, not fighters.

One of the men on the detail named Keith was from Chicago. We had gone through both basic training and advanced training together, and we had become friends. Another guy from Washington State named Orin became a close friend also. Then there was the man from Toledo who joined our inner circle. I can't remember his real name, but we all called him "Pop" because he was twenty-four years old, and that made him ancient to the rest of us. The four of us plus a few more men headed to the motor pool. There was no sound of gunfire, meaning the base was not under attack, so we were left to wonder what the lieutenant was about lead us into.

Lieutenant Fuzz was waiting beside his Jeep for us at the motor pool. He was wearing his helmet and had a .45 strapped to his right side. There were also two 3/4-ton trucks parked next to his Jeep. The two drivers were wearing their helmets, but they had no weapons. We stood at attention with our rifle butts on the ground as he briefed us. He said that the company commander, the old man, wanted his headquarters building spruced up with new landscaping and that we were going to drive through a village or two outside the base and find some plants for the headquarters building. We threw a few shovels in the back of the trucks and got in. The trucks had canvas tops, and we sat on wooden benches under the canvas. He told the drivers to stay several yards apart for safety. Then we headed out on our important mission to find some plants as we followed Lieutenant Fuzz's Jeep.

We passed through the main gate to the base and turned right onto a dirt road. There were agriculture fields on the left with mountains in the distance. The base perimeter contained by a barbed wire fence was on our right. For the first time I could see the entire runway that we had landed on just a couple nights before in the mass confusion of an attack. All was peaceful now as we saw men working on aircraft in the hangars and workshops in the far distance. Olive drab-colored helicopters and planes were taking off and landing. I noticed that each had their own unique sounds, and over the next few months, I would be able to identify the different types of aircraft by these sounds as well as if they were taking off or landing without seeing them.

We followed Lieutenant Fuzz's Jeep another few miles, and he turned left onto another dirt road. We were passing rice fields on both sides of us which were full of farmers and water buffaloes hard at work. After a couple more miles, we passed through a thicket of trees and came upon a small village of thatched-roof huts. We stopped, and Lieutenant Fuzz ordered four guys to get the shovels out and start digging up all the banana trees they could find. Our mission had begun. I along with three others were ordered to guard those who were digging.

Within a short time, several Vietnamese men and women came charging out of the huts to see what was going on. None of them were armed. I could clearly see the anger in their faces. Their only weapons were anger and curses. We raised our weapons and they stopped, but if they hadn't stopped, I probably would have shot one of them in the chest. There was no emotion involved. It was how I was trained to react, and it was like I was on autopilot. None of us fired a shot, but the damage had been done. They hated us. We were the mighty US Army, and they were helpless in keeping us from taking their property. We could do anything we wanted to do.

After loading the banana plants into the back of the trucks, we headed back to the base to plant them around our headquarters so it would look better, and the old man would be happy. I later felt guilty and wondered how I could have come so close to ending a man's life over a few banana trees. I remember thinking at the time that what we had just done was obviously wrong, but I was in the Army and had to obey my orders.

VIGNETTE SIX

NHA TRANG AIR BASE

I SPENT A FULL YEAR AT THE NHA TRANG Air Base during the Vietnam War. Nha Trang was not one of those front-line bases of the war. It was considered a safe base used for aircraft repair and maintenance. My unit did all the required work on the aircraft. We worked on both rotary wing and fixed wing Army aircraft used in the war. The 5th Special Forces, Green Berets, were also based in Nha Trang. We depended on the infantry soldiers to protect us and the air base from attacks by the Viet Cong, communist guerilla fighters, in the surrounding mountains, but that didn't keep the base from being attacked every other week or two.

The attacks always seemed to come at two or three o'clock in the morning. We would awake to explosions and gunfire, quickly get dressed, then run to our assigned sandbag bunkers with our weapons and await orders. At times, we would see a parked helicopter or two on fire, flairs would be illuminating the night sky, and Puff the Magic Dragon, a war plane, would be spewing red tipped tracer bullets from its Gatling guns. The tracer bullets looked like red water pouring from a water hose being sprayed on the mountain side. Usually within an hour the all-clear was given and we would go back to our barracks.

In addition to our regular jobs, everyone was assigned guard duty from time to time, either at the airbase or at the large fuel storage tanks located about a half mile from the base. I was assigned to guard one of the large hangars once. I walked around the hangar in the dark all night long with my weapon at the ready position. About midnight, I began hearing gunfire in the distance. I didn't see anything, but spent bullets began falling all around me, hitting the concrete pavement like rain drops. They must have been shot from a very long distance because they didn't have enough velocity left to do any damage by the time they got to me. They just fell harmlessly to the ground. I saved one of the bullets and wore it on my dog tags until I got out of the Army.

Another time I was assigned guard duty at the fuel depot. I along with three other Americans and four Chinese mercenaries were assigned to guard the facility for twenty-four hours. We were commanded by a Vietnamese Army lieutenant. He selected two Americans to walk around the complex clockwise fifteen minutes apart. Then two mercenaries were to walk counterclockwise around the complex fifteen minutes apart. So, two Americans and two mercenaries were guarding the tanks at the same time for twenty-four hours. We were just inside a ten-foot-high concertina barbed wire fence. I remembered that it took an hour to complete the circle so every fifteen minutes someone was passing every part of the complex. Whenever I passed a mercenary heading in the opposite direction, we would just nod at each other since neither of us knew the other's language. Every two hours we changed guards.

On the north side of the fuel depot was a small thatched-roof hooch village. Every time I passed by, the village kids would throw rocks over the fence at me. I was never hit, but that didn't keep their parents from laughing at me. I thought we were there to protect them. The rest of the area outside of the fence was a dense, dark jungle. I couldn't see more than two or three feet into the jungle. As I was about to wrap up my second lap, I heard twigs snapping. It sounded like someone was sneaking right up to me. I lifted my rifle and aimed into the jungle toward the sound not more than fifteen feet away from me. We were trained to shoot first and ask questions later. I had my finger on the trigger and was about to squeeze it when a goat's head came into sight. I lowered my weapon.

I saved the Army about $2,000.00 by not accidentally shooting the goat. Livestock was the livelihood of the Vietnamese farmers, and we were told that the government compensated them for collateral damage to their animals, yet accidentally shooting a civilian cost the government nothing. Like they say, "War is hell."

VIGNETTE SEVEN

ROTATING INTO MY JOB SLOT

AS SLOTS BEGAN TO OPEN UP AND WERE being filled, Lieutenant Fuzz's detail unit got smaller and smaller. It began with about twenty or twenty-five of us, but it dwindled down fast. Over the next few days, he had a variety of jobs for us who were left on detail duty, but there was none more important than stealing those banana trees from small villages and planting them around the 339th headquarters building.

I spent one day painting the exterior of one of the barracks white. I also had the opportunity to paint the stones circling the flagpole and the ones circling the bulletin board in front of the headquarters building. For some reason the Army required all stones on their bases to be painted white.

Another day, we hauled truckloads of trash to an open dump a few miles away from the air base. There were four of us on each truck, the driver and three of us riding in the back with the trash. We were all fully armed. As we arrived at the dump, I was surprised at how many Vietnamese ran up to the trucks before the trucks could even stop – men, women, and children. They wanted to be the first to find something in the trucks to salvage. It was difficult to back the trucks up without running over them. They reminded me of vultures attacking a dead deer on the side of the road. They swarmed us. Some even climbed into the truck beds as the trucks were still backing up. It didn't take very long to clean out the trucks and leave.

We were passing through a jungle area when returning to the air base when several gunshots rang out in quick order. *Pow! Pow! Pow! Pow!* We didn't see anybody, but they obviously weren't far away. The three of us riding in the back immediately hit the deck of the truck bed. The drivers were wise enough to hit the gas petal and keep going. We never saw the shooters, and we all returned to the base safely, but it was a good reminder that we were, after all, in a war zone.

Eventually my slot opened up, and I began working eight-hour shifts as an aircraft repairman in the largest hangar on base. The main hangar had several different repair shops such as sheet metal, engine, avionics, electrical, hydraulics, and instrumentation to name a few. One thing that I was surprised to learn was that a large amount of damage to the helicopters we were working on was caused by human error and not the war. I was told that most of the young helicopter pilots were arriving in Vietnam with as little as eight weeks of training and very little experience flying. We had young pilots who would take off, lift their helicopters a few feet into the air, and then flip them over crashing them back to the ground upside down. I remember once when a pilot flew off in his helicopter, completed his mission, and made it back to the airfield, but crashed it as he landed. He tried to land in a space between two parked helicopters. The problem was that there wasn't enough room between the two parked ones to land, and he damaged three helicopters including his own. The fixed-wing aircraft pilots were much better trained and experienced, and we didn't see much pilot damage to their planes.

We aircraft repairmen only had about eight weeks of training ourselves before arriving in Vietnam. We definitely were not experts, but we had thick green repair manuals for every possible repair problem or maintenance situation facing us, with step-by-step instructions as well as large diagrams that we followed. After a repair was completed, a highly experienced technical sergeant would inspect the work we did and, if correct, would put his literal stamp of approval on the repair or replaced part. The stamp included his name and date. There were also civilian Bell helicopter mechanics on base to help us. The Army required that after a repair was completed, one repairman from among those working on it was required to ride on the test flight. That ensured that we did our best work. I had my share of test flights, and I had a couple of harrowing experiences on those test flights. I've become aware that God was protecting me more than I realized He was at the time I was in Vietnam.

VIGNETTE NUMBER EIGHT
TEST FLIGHTS

A HELICOPTER THAT I HAD WORKED ON was revving up its engine as it sat on the taxiway. The top rotor and the tail rotor were both spinning at top speed. The pilot was readying for a test flight when I realized it was my time to go along on the test flight. I sprinted out to the helicopter with my head lowered and jumped into the passenger area. We had taken out the passenger seats for better access to the work area, and the rear doors were fixed open. I sat down on the floor. The pilots saw me enter, and they took off. We rose several feet vertically before slowly moving forward. The nose of the helicopter lowered slightly so the top rotors could bite into the air and propel us forward. We rose like a plane slowly taking off. The rhythmic *thump, thump, thump* sound of the top rotors rotating against the air resistance was always music to my ears. I still love the sound they make when helicopters from nearby Fort Bragg fly over our house today.

The pilot ran through several maneuvers without any problems. Then without warning, he banked sharply to the left. The helicopter was at about a thirty-degree angle as it made the turn. Suddenly, I was looking straight down at the ground as I began slowly sliding across the floor to the open door. I grabbed a couple seat attachment ring pins in the floor with my index fingers and held on for dear life. The pilot immediately realized what was happening, and he leveled the helicopter. I was safe, the helicopter passed its test flight, and I learned to never ride in a helicopter without seats again.

A few months later, I was aboard another test flight. This time I was safely sitting on the back seat with the doors closed. The flight was uneventful for the first few minutes as the pilot went through his maneuvers. Suddenly, the engine quit running, and it got very quiet. We began descending – straight down. A plane could have glided down without its engine, but not a helicopter. I could hear the pilots discussing the situation while trying to stay calm. They were flipping switches off and on. We were auto-rotating down to the ground from a couple thousand feet in the air. That meant that as we came down, the air resistance was slowly rotating the top rotors and slowing our descent. I remember from advanced training that the crash would be a so-called "survivable crash." That meant that we would most likely not be killed, but would sustain serious injuries. As I was reliving the good and the bad in my life, the engine suddenly started back up again. We were a just few hundred feet above the ground. The pilot was able to regain control of the helicopter, and we landed safely on the tarmac.

As I recall helicopter flights from over fifty years ago, there's a more tragic memory that comes to mind. While working in the hangar one day, I heard a UH1B Huey returning to the airbase. This occurred so often each day that I normally would not have even noticed, but for some reason I did that time. I saw the helicopter coming in from the mountains, and something was hanging beneath it. As it neared, I couldn't believe what I saw. There, hanging by his neck, was a man. His hands were tied behind his back, and he was blindfolded. The site horrified me. The helicopter passed the hangar and headed toward the end of the tarmac. I had heard over and over again about war being hell, but this really shocked me into the reality of what could happen during a war.

A couple days later, I talked to someone who had a ride on that very flight. He said that the Special Forces were bringing two captured Viet Cong soldiers in for interrogation. The two prisoners were squatting on the floor of the helicopter. He said that their arms were tightly tied behind their backs, and they were blindfolded. He said that there were two Special Forces soldiers and a regular south Vietnamese Army interrogator on board. The interrogator was asking the prisoners questions, and when they wouldn't tell him anything, he tied a rope around one of their necks and calmly kicked the man out of the helicopter. The man screamed for only a couple of seconds before his life suddenly ended. My friend said that he felt a slight jolt to the helicopter as the man's weight reached the end of the rope. He said that the other prisoner began talking nonstop. I don't know how the story ended for that Viet Cong prisoner.

I'm reminded that even though I was stationed at a safe base in Vietnam, I still saw some horrific things during my year in Vietnam. I can't even image what horrors our soldiers fighting in the jungles experienced.

VIGNETTE NINE

MALARIA AND HALLUCINATIONS

EVERY MONDAY MORNING AFTER BREAK-fast was malaria pill time. We all lined up in single file outside of the dispensary. At the head of the line would be a large metal pot of water sitting on a wooden bench. A medic would give each of us two malaria pills, we would dip a metal cup into the pot of water, take a sip with our pills, then we passed the cup to the next person in line. Yes, we all drank from the same cup without any cleaning of the cup. It wasn't very sanitary, but none of us caught malaria.

On our times off, after work hours, or on weekends, we had two places we could go off base: the white sandy beach on the South China Sea or downtown Nha Trang. My friends and I saw two American women at the beach once not much older than us sunbathing on beach blankets. The only women in the army at that time were the nurses at the field hospitals, and they were all lieutenants or captains. As officers, they were forbidden to associate with enlisted men like us, but my friend Keith considered himself a lady's man and walked over to start up a conversation with them... That turned out to be a big mistake. I've never heard so much profanity coming from a woman's mouth or even from a drunken sailor's mouth before. They really put him in his place.

Just as the beach was a very safe place for US soldiers to visit, so was downtown Nha Trang. We would go there unarmed and usually dressed in civilian clothes. For some reason, Nha Trang was untouched by the war raging in most other parts of the country. It wasn't a very big city, but it was a bustling city. The streets were busy with cars, motorbikes, rickshaws, and pedestrians. There were sidewalk vendors and artists. The main street through town had rows of old concrete buildings attached to each other along both sides. None of the buildings were more than three or four stories tall. Most had sloped, faded red tile roofs, but some had flat roofs or roof terraces. Many had balconies on their fronts and were probably built during the French occupation during the early 1900's.

There was a United Service Organization (USO) on one corner where we occasionally hung out. I remember there was always a Vietnamese military policeman standing just outside the front door. Once we went downtown to celebrate the birthday of our friend Pops. He was turning twenty-five years old. We visited several shops including an Indian tailor shop where each of us was fitted for tailor-made suits to be picked up at a later date. They cost no more than $20.00 a piece. I also ordered a pair of bearskin shoes.

28

We ended up at a French restaurant located on the roof terrace of a four-story building. I can't remember what we ate, but I do remember the drinks we had. My friends all ordered beers, but since I didn't drink alcohol, I ordered a Vietnamese tea... That turned out to be a big mistake for me. At the end of the meal, I began to hallucinate. I remember walking over to the edge of the roof terrace and looking down at the busy street below. I was Superman, and I was going to jump off the roof and fly over the heads of those below. Keith recognized that something was wrong with me, grabbed my arm, and led me back to the table. I had been drugged.

They got me back to the base okay, and the next morning I was back to normal. I can remember during in-country processing back at Tent City in Saigon months before that we were warned spies were drugging soldiers who were off duty and trying to gather personal information from them. I had been lucky.

VIGNETTE TEN
R & R AND COMMAND SESSIONS

I HAD BEEN WORKING AT THE HANGAR for several months and the jobs and test flights had become routine. Some weeks we got more aircraft in for repairs than we could handle during our eight-hour workdays. There was a time when we were working twelve-hour shifts around the clock. We still had the occasional early morning attacks, but nothing major and certainly nothing like the full-blown battle that greeted me that first night in Nha Trang. Apparently, the Viet Cong just wanted to remind us that they were watching us to keep us a little edgy. The weeks-long monsoon rains made everything muddy and slippery, but the rains eventually stopped. The rain caused us to work in our ponchos at times which made everything very difficult.

At the sixth month of my deployment in a war zone, I was scheduled to go on R & R. I had a choice of a five-day trip to either Bangkok, Thailand, Hong Kong, or a city in Australia that I have forgotten. I chose Hong Kong as did a couple of my friends. We flew out of Saigon on a

commercial flight. The landing at the old Hong Kong airport back then was a nail-biting experience. Not only did
the pilot have to weave his way through tall mountains to
get to the runway, but through skyscrapers, as well. The
airport seemed to be located in the middle of the city, but
we landed safely.

We were given private rooms paid for by our government at the Presidential Hotel in Kowloon. We shopped
in downtown Hong Kong and bought souvenirs for our
family members back home. I remember buying my
mother an ivory carving of a Chinese junk that had a
man standing up on the deck with a pole. We took a tour
bus to a walled city which was occupied only by women
and children. We were told that all the men worked at
hotels in London and seldom came home. We also saw
the boat used in the award-winning movie *The World
of Suzi Wong*. Then there was the outdoor fish market
with thousands of fish drying in the sun on bamboo mats.
One night before leaving, we ate dinner and watched a
musical show at the Hong Kong Playboy Club. I can't
recall what we ate there, but I do remember that all of the
waitresses had rabbit ears and bunny tails.

The five days of R & R passed by quickly, and then we
were back to our regular job routines at the air base. Our
company commander occasionally held "command information sessions" at our makeshift amphitheater near one
end of the base. I remember that he was a major, but I
forgot his name. He would stand on the stage and give

us an update on how the war was going and how our unit was contributing to the cause.

Then he allowed us to ask him any questions we wanted. I only remember two questions, and his answers. The first question was, "How much was the war costing the US government?" Without blinking an eye, he told us $14,000,000.00 a day and 600 lives a week. That was a lot of money back then, and I couldn't comprehend the loss of so many young men, most of them around twenty years old like me. The second question was, "Why are we fighting this war?" He answered candidly that officially it was the need for us to stop communism from spreading throughout the southeast Asian countries before it could spread to The Philippines. Unofficially, he said it was to test the military's ability to fight a war with helicopters, a new concept at the time, so that we would be prepared to fight the Russians in the future. Basically, he was saying it was a practice war, and the costs didn't really matter.

That makeshift amphitheater was also used for entertainment. Every couple of months or so, a no-name band with dancing go-go girls from the States would put on a show. They were usually pretty good concerts, but nothing to write home about. Then there was the time when word got around the base that the USO was bringing celebrities in to perform at the amphitheater that Friday evening. Speculation was that it would be Bob Hope with either Ann Margaret or Raquel Welch. We heard that they were putting on shows at another base, and we just assumed it would be those stars. There were approximately 500 soldiers who showed up, and there was standing room only. Most had been drinking beer, and it was getting a little loud and lively. We all had our instamatic cameras ready.

At showtime, a helicopter landed nearby, and we knew it had to be the stars! A middle-aged woman got out of the helicopter and walked the short distance to the stage. There were a couple USO officials with her. There was no Bob Hope to be seen, and the woman definitely was not Ann Margaret or Raquel Welch. An army captain welcomed her to the Nha Trang Airfield, then he told us to give a big round of applause to the "big mouth of comedy, Martha Ray." I then remembered seeing her before on the *Johnny Carson Show*. She was very funny, and she went through several comedy routines for an hour or two before she flew away, but she was nothing to write home about either.

VIGNETTE ELEVEN
COMBAT SOLDIERS

AS I MENTIONED BEFORE, NHA TRANG was the headquarters of the 5th Special Forces, Green Berets, but American soldiers weren't the only ones stationed there. We were the majority, but several other countries were also represented. There were small forces of Australian Special Forces and South Korean Marines. The South Vietnamese Air Force flew prop planes in and out of the air base and had headquarters there. There were also Chinese mercenaries.

But the craziest group of soldiers based there were the South Vietnamese Special Forces. They wore black berets, and we called them "cowboys" because they were so wild and undisciplined. Whenever they returned to base from field missions, we could count on there being some serious trouble. All of the forces returning from combat missions would hit the bars downtown. There they could relax and unwind and forget about the war they were fighting for a while. The barmaids served Saigon teas, small glasses of watered-down liquor, and preferred sitting and talking with the Americans or Australians. The barmaid's job, after all, was to keep the customers buying more and more drinks, so they spent most of their time with the guys who had the money to spend over the poorly paid cowboys. The cowboys resented being overlooked by the barmaids and always, *always* started trouble. Free-for-all brawls would break out in the bars whenever the cowboys and the Green Berets were back at base at the same time. On the battlefield, they were fighting together to defeat a common enemy, but in town, they hated each other. The South Viennese military police would have to come in and break up the fights. It got so bad that it was decided by the commanders that whenever the cowboys and Special Forces were back from the field at the same time, they could not be in the bars at the same time. That solved that problem.

At the other end of the spectrum were the South Korean Marines. In addition to their military training, they were all highly skilled in Taekwondo. They practiced self-discipline and never, *never* caused any problems when they came back from the battlefield. One thing that I did notice about them was that they seldom showed any outer emotions or facial expressions. Once, one of our guys was on a flight to bring some of them back to the base. He said so many of them tried to board the helicopter that there wasn't enough room for all of them inside, and they couldn't close the doors. Two or three Marines stood outside of the helicopter on the landing skids and held on for dear life to anything they could grab as they flew back. Unfortunately, one of them lost his grip and fell to his death. None of the others who witnessed what happened said anything or even showed any kind of emotion.

There was a soldier in our unit I occasionally ate lunch with. He wasn't a close friend, but he worked in the same hangar that I did. I can't recall his name, but he was very outgoing and was always joking around, always the life of the party. Everybody liked him. He began telling us that he was bored with his job. There just wasn't enough action for him repairing helicopters. He said that as long as he was in Vietnam, he wanted to be where the action was. He began asking his platoon leader to get him transferred to an infantry unit. The company commander eventually granted his request, but the standards and qualifications of the elite Green Berets were way too high for him to join them. He left our unit and ended up with a Vietnamese cowboy unit. He wore one of their signature black berets, and he was deployed on combat missions with them.

I was told that he was no longer the same happy-go-lucky guy that he used to be by someone who saw him once in the PX. It was a few weeks later that I saw him myself returning from a mission. His jungle fatigues were filthy. He had a heavy camouflaged backpack on his shoulders, and he was carrying by its handle an M16 rifle. At the time, they were issued only to infantry units. We non-combat soldiers had been issued the older and heavier M14s which didn't have handles. He had a beard, and he smelled bad. I remember that his eyes were haunting and he had a fixed expression on his face of disbelief or terror. He did speak to us, but he didn't have much to say as he walked on by. That was the last time I saw him, and I never heard anything about him again. I have thought about him occasionally over the past fifty-five years, and I wonder if he ever made it back home.

VIGNETTE TWELVE

SHORT-TIMERS FEVER

THERE IS A STORY I MUST SLIP IN HERE about the time a Vietnamese civilian working at the base stole my radio and left the music behind.

I was tired because we had been working twelve-hour shifts, so I went to a break area to lay down on a couch. My PX-purchased radio was resting on a ledge next to me playing American 1960's music on Armed Forces Radio. This was about two years before Pat Sajak became the disc jockey on Armed Forces Radio (folks probably remember that Robin Williams played Pat's character in the movie, *Good Morning Vietnam*).

Before I knew it, a buddy nudged me awake and told me someone was taking my radio. I jumped up and saw a Vietnamese civilian quickly backing away with my radio. I noticed he was constantly turning the volume up louder and louder as he did, taking the radio, but leaving the music behind hoping I wouldn't notice. When he saw me, he turned and ran to a motorized taxi scooter. He had hidden it under the seat, but I was able to find it and get my music back.

Sometime during the month of April in 1967, I came down with "short-timer's fever. Short-timers were soldiers who had three months or less on their twelve-month Vietnam deployment. They would make calendars with ninety boxes and X out each box as the days passed by until they went home. I heard that many short-timer infantry soldiers who had been fighting for months became super-stitious. They became less aggressive and much more cautious as their days passed by and never volunteered for anything again. For me, I had a bad case of it. I had only ninety days left in Vietnam, and I was looking forward to catching that commercial airplane in Saigon and flying home. I made a short-timers calendar and I hung it on my locker door, but the days just seemed to get longer, and they passed by more and more slowly.

As I mentioned before, the infantry soldiers fighting in the field became short-timers, and some of them became superstitious. They believed that their luck was running out. They would no longer volunteer for dangerous mis-sions or take unnecessary risks. They wanted to make sure that after nine months of firefights in the jungles without being shot that they didn't get killed or wounded during their last ninety days. That made a lot of sense to me back then, and it still does today. I just continued going about my routine job up to my last day. Our replace-ments were already on base and were working on detail duty, waiting for their slots to open up. Lieutenant Fuzz had been replaced and had left Vietnam months earlier.

I received many letters during that year I was in Vietnam. Many were from members of my church who I didn't even know. A few of us who grew up in the church, including the pastor's son, were serving in Vietnam, and a group of women made it a point that we always had some mail at mail-call. My mother wrote to me often. I remember that she always wrote a Bible verse on the back of the enve-lopes. I also wrote home often. For some reason, I never received a letter from my father. He just didn't write letters, but I knew he was continually praying for my safety. When I returned home, he placed an article in the Memphis evening paper and publicly thanked God for bringing me home safely. I still have a clipping of that article in one of my Vietnam photo albums upstairs.

Finally, my last day arrived. There was no going- away party or celebration because every day soldiers were coming in and going out. It meant nothing to anybody except for those who were leaving. I don't remember how we got back to Saigon, but we were finally flying back home on a Pan Am 707. Everybody was excited, laughing, and talking loudly. The mood on the plane was the exact opposite of the mood a year before while flying into Vietnam. We were all wearing our short-sleeved dress khakis. I had my specialist rank patches on each sleeve. My rifle marksman metal was pinned on the left side of my shirt just under my name tag. On the right side were the four ribbons I was awarded in Vietnam.

No, I didn't earn any of them by risking my life to save someone else or by doing anything heroic. I was a helicopter mechanic, but I did receive The National Defense Service Metal, The Vietnam Service Metal, The Vietnam Campaign Metal, and a Good Conduct Metal. Everyone else on board the plane had the same metals that I had, but I wore them proudly. I realize that was the Army's way of thanking us for our service.

VIGNETTE THIRTEEN
HOMEWARD BOUND

THE FLIGHT BACK TO MEMPHIS TOOK about twenty-two hours. We were well fed on the plane and the drinks began flowing. Some soldiers broke out in song whether they had any singing ability or not. Back then, smoking was allowed on flights and several soldiers were smoking cigars. After all, they had accomplished a great feat by returning home from Vietnam alive. It was party time! The noisy cabin became a little smoky. The young, attractive stewardesses began flirting with us. I don't think anyone slept during the entire flight. We made refueling stops in Japan and the Philippines before arriving in Seattle where we changed planes. There was another stop in Chicago before I landed in Memphis.

My three close friends who were with me throughout my year in Vietnam went their separate ways. Orin lived in Kirkland, Washington, and got off in Seattle. I would never see him again. He wasn't going to Fort Knox, but to a base on the West Coast. Keith was from Chicago and got off there. Pops changed planes in Chicago and flew home to Toledo, Ohio. But the three of us would meet together again two weeks later. We were out of Vietnam, but we weren't out of the Army yet.

If I remember correctly, I arrived at the Memphis airport in the early afternoon hours. Back then, decades before 9/11 caused the creation of the TSA, anybody could enter the airport at any time and walk right up to any gate. I remember that my mother was at the gate waiting for me as I exited the plane. I had trouble remembering who else was there with her. After contacting my siblings, they reminded me that both of my sisters, Sharon and Lois, as well as my brother, Robert, who was about seven years old at the time, were there to welcome me home. One of my aunts was there, as well. My father and older brother, Paul, were working.

My mother began crying and couldn't say anything, but she did hug and kiss me. She then grabbed my left hand and we walked through the long terminal together and out to the car without saying a word. A little over twenty-three years earlier, she had welcomed my soldier father home from France. I could tell that she was not only relieved that I was safely home, but that she was also very proud of me. It was like she was walking through the airport showing me off in my uniform with my five metals. I don't remember what happened when we got home that day, but a day or two later, they took pictures of me in my Army uniform with Paul in his fireman's uniform. I spent the next few days spending time with friends and family. I also attended Chi Alpha, a student religious organization at Memphis State University, with my sister. It was there I made several new Christian friends.

After my fourteen-day leave was up, I rode a Greyhound bus to my next duty station at Fort Knox, Kentucky. There I joined back up with my remaining two good Vietnam friends, Keith and the "old man." There along with several other returning soldiers, we were assigned to detail duty for the remainder of our service time which was about six months. The duty officer was very easy on us returning soldiers. We did a little grounds keeping from time to time, but mostly we just stoked the coal-burning furnaces as the Kentucky winter began to set in. There were no helicopter repair job slots for us to fill at Fort Knox. It was an infantry training center at the time we were there, and we weren't infantry. We were still helicopter repairmen. The barracks we stayed in were built prior to World War II and were not insulated. They had these large coal-fed furnaces in their basements that kept each barracks warm. We basically kept the fires burning by shoveling coal into them as needed. After doing that, we were basically on our own during the rest of the day. I realized during these last few weeks the Army was feeding us and paying us to perform very little or no work at all.

VIGNETTE FOURTEEN
LIFE AT FORT KNOX

WE HAD BEEN AT FORT KNOX A FEW WEEKS and had our daily routines down pat: wake up, eat breakfast, add coal to the furnaces, goof off until lunch, eat lunch, check the furnaces, goof off until dinner, eat dinner, check the furnaces again, then goof off until bedtime. The next morning it would begin all over again. To be honest, I'm exaggerating when I say "goof off." A better word would have been "explore."

Fort Knox was a sprawling base with lots of areas to explore. There was a huge PX that not only sold the basics like food, drinks, and toiletries, but it also had a book section and a camera section with a large selection of the best cameras at that time. I bought a 35mm Petri camera. We could buy furniture and lamps. There was an electronics section which sold stereos, radios, and televisions where Keith bought a reel-to-reel tape recorder. They even sold motorcycles and motor scooters. It was like a mall, and we spent a lot of time there.

At another area of the base was the General Patton Museum which I found intriguing. As is known, he commanded the American armor divisions in Northern Africa and Western Europe during World War II. There were several different types of tanks on display, some of them camouflaged. What I enjoyed most were the battlefield models of some of his greatest battles, showing locations of the German and American positions with small model tanks.

There was the United States Bullion Depository where billions of dollars' worth of gold bricks are stored. When we hear the words "Fort Knox", that's what most people think of. If I remember correctly, there were no trees or buildings within 100 yards to any side of the building, only grass. There was a chain link fence topped with barbed wire at the perimeter. There were no guards visible that we could see. Of course, we couldn't get inside the fence, but it was interesting just to see the building.

We also watched movies on base and spent time in the company rec room watching TV and playing pool. I wanted to buy a car, either a Mustang or a Plymouth Road Runner. I had sold my 1955 Chevrolet to my brother when I got drafted. It only took a few months before his wife wrecked it. Fort Knox was the first place where I could actually have a car on base. Keith had bought a new white Camaro and Pops had his 1962 Corvette. I needed a car. I asked the duty officer for a pass to go home for three days, and he granted my request. I caught a Greyhound bus and headed home.

On the bus, I sat two seats behind a cute young brunette. I thought we had made eye contact when I first got on the bus, but I wasn't sure. I was still a shy introvert, but when the person sitting next to her got off the bus, I moved up and sat next to her. Her first words to me were, "Are you a soldier?" I was wearing civilian clothes, and I asked how she knew. She said she could just tell. We talked until she got off at Cave City, a small town about sixty miles south of Fort Knox. I told her that I was from Memphis and that I had recently returned from Vietnam. She was impressed. I didn't tell her I was only a helicopter repairman, and she never asked what I did there. She said that she was working in Louisville as a secretary and was renting a room there with two other girls. She lived in Cave City and took the bus home every weekend. I can't remember her name now, but before she got off the bus, I had her phone number. She told me to call her sometime. I couldn't believe my good luck.

The bus continued down I-65. Back then, I-65 was called the Dixie Highway and nicknamed the "Dixie Dieway." Every year or two, a drunk soldier would die in a wreck going to or coming from Louisville which was about forty miles north of the base. The bus stopped at several small towns along the way, picking up passengers or letting some off. We passed the exit to Mammoth Cave and went through the small town of Boiling Springs before turning west at Nashville onto I-40. From there, home was about four hours away. I can remember that I could hardly wait to get back to the base and call the girl's number to see if my luck was for real or not.

VIGNETTE FIFTEEN
GIRLS AND CARS

MY DAD AND I WENT CAR SHOPPING. WE never made it to the Plymouth dealership, but we did visit a nearby Ford dealership. There were rows and rows of new 1968 Mustangs in several color choices, and I picked one out in candy apple red. My dad had always paid cash for everything he ever bought including cars. Each month that I was in Vietnam, I sent my extra combat pay home for savings. The cost of the Mustang was $2,200.00, and I was a few hundred dollars short. My dad chipped in the rest, and we paid cash. Before heading back to the base, I drove around Memphis showing off my new car to family and friends. I left Memphis after church that Sunday and headed back to Fort Knox in my brand-new Mustang. The trip was uneventful, but I stopped a couple times along the way to walk around the car. I just wanted to be sure that everything was okay.

Back at the base, we continued our daily routine. I decided to find out if the phone number I got from the girl on the bus was her real number before telling my friends about it.

I didn't want to look like a fool. There was a row of phone booths outside the rec center. I put a dime into the coin slot, held my breath, and dialed the number on the rotary dial. After a couple of rings, she answered. We talked for a while, and she asked if I wanted to come to Louisville to see her. Yes! I asked her if I could bring a couple friends with me. She said both of her roommates were home, and that was fine.

We took my new Mustang and drove for about an hour to get to Louisville and to find her boarding house. Once we did, she came out with her two roommates. They were both cute and friendly, so my two friends were very pleased. We didn't know any girls in Kentucky until I made that bus trip. I still can't remember any of the girls' names. All six of us got into my Mustang with Pops and two girls in the back seat and my girl sat on the console between me and Keith. She gave me directions to a restaurant that they liked. There, we ate and got to know each other better. Everyone was happy with the person they ended up with, including me and my original girl. We all got back into my car after dinner sitting as we had before. Directing me from her seat on the console, my girl showed us around Louisville as I drove. It was a fun night because my friends and I had never been there before. Later we dropped them off at their boarding house and headed back to base. We met them a couple more times later before going our separate ways.

It was wintertime, and back at the base we shoveled tons of coal. A couple of weeks before Christmas, Keith invited

Pops and me to his parents' home in Chicago for the weekend. We piled into his new Camaro and headed out in the falling snow. The trip was slow, but we made it safely. While there, we walked down Lake Shore Drive looking at all of the automated Christmas windows. The wind was blowing off Lake Michigan, and I thought that I would freeze to death. We also went to the top of the 100-story John Hancock Building which had recently been completed. The view from there was fantastic, but they were having trouble keeping glass in the upper floor windows. The high winds were sucking the glass out of their frames. I heard that they had solved the problem later. I was planning on studying architecture after getting out of the Army, and I was impressed by the height and design of the building. It tapered on all four sides as it went up, and there was massive steel X-bracing on the exterior. We took pictures of the Picasso sculpture on the ground near the main entrance.

We made it safely back to the base on Sunday evening. Monday morning, we were back to our daily routine. I realize that my final four or five months in the Army were actually fun times.

VIGNETTE SIXTEEN
PARTY TIME

ANOTHER SOLDIER I BARELY KNEW JOINED our group. He had been working with Pops shoveling coal for the furnaces. I don't remember what his name was, but he was from either Virginia or West Virginia. He was a tall, lanky red head. I didn't like him because I found him to be loud and obnoxious. He didn't have a car, and I believe that's why he began hanging out with us. I was a professing Christian at the time, but I'm ashamed to admit that nobody could have known that by looking at my life. My friends liked to drink and party, and I liked being with them. I was always the designated driver because I never drank anything stronger than a 7Up.

Once we were partying at a bar in a small town on the Dixie Highway named Elizabethtown. The bar was popular with soldiers and was packed that night. The music was loud, and everyone was partying. After we had been there a while, a bouncer came up to me and said that I would have to leave. I was getting kicked out of the bar. I had only been drinking 7Up. My friends who were enjoying their Falstaff and Stroh beers could stay. I went out and sat in my car. To this day, I cannot remember what my offense was. The others soon came out, and I safely drove them back to the base. I possibly saved their lives by doing all the driving. I had unknowingly become an Uber driver decades before there were any. My friends never let me forget about getting kicked out of that bar that night.

Another time we were partying at a different bar on the Dixie Highway and I was, again, drinking 7Up while the other three enjoyed their beers. There was a pretty good band composed of soldiers from the base playing songs from The Beatles and The Doors. It was getting smoky and loud. The red-headed guy was consuming lots of beers and was getting a bit loud and rowdy, but no bouncer came up to him and told him to leave. He began to get sick and wanted to leave. The night was young, but we decided to leave and get him back to the base because he had no other way to get back.

I had only driven a short distance from the bar when the redhead threw up all over the back seat of my new Mustang. I didn't even like this guy to start with; now I hated him. I was mad and pulled over at a gas station. Keith and Pops got him out of the car and got him to lie down on a wooden bench. Then they began cleaning up the mess with paper towels and water from the gas station's bathroom. I sat there watching them wondering if my car would ever be the same again. Pops bought some air freshener and sprayed it into the car. They did a good job of cleaning up, but it was a while before my car had the new car smell again. The red-headed guy never rode in my car again.

It was 1968, and we would be discharged from the Army in mid-February. The two years had passed by quickly. During that time, I had traveled halfway around the world and back and had seen a war from the safety of Nha Trang. I had met some good people along the way, but I was no longer the same person I was before joining the Army. That bothered me. On February 17, 1968, I received my DD214 form, and I was honorably discharged from the Army. I was now free to return home. We packed our cars and said our goodbyes. Keith had a phone installations job with Ma Bell waiting for him back in Chicago. Pops was a mechanic at a Ford dealership in Toledo before the war, and he went back to his old job. I would never see or talk to them again. Before I got drafted, I was working as a cashier at the largest supermarket in Memphis which was located in mid-town. There were no scanners back then, and we had to punch in the price of each item with our fingers. The supermarket had held my job open for me, and I picked right back up where I had left off. I continued working there as my life was quickly getting back to normal.

The next phase of my life was about to begin. I had always wanted to be an architect, and my first step to reach that goal was to enroll at State Technical Institute at Memphis and begin studying architecture.

VIGNETTE SEVENTEEN
LIFE GOES ON

AS I'VE MENTIONED A COUPLE OF TIMES before, it has been over fifty-three years since I was in the Army and served in Vietnam, but in March of 2018, Vietnam began to haunt me again.

I was diagnosed with a rare cancer called Liposarcoma which had been growing in my abdomen for decades without my knowing it. It was a very large tumor, fifteen pounds, and it was removed in one piece during a six-hour surgery at the UNC Hospital in Chapel Hill, North Carolina. The surgeon took pictures of it to show me how big it really was. I was born with only one kidney, and that one kidney was also removed during the surgery because it was encapsulated in the cancer. That caused me to rely on dialysis three days a week for four hours a day just to stay alive.

The Veteran's Administration determined soon after the operation that exposure to Agent Orange in Vietnam five decades ago was most likely the cause of my slow-growing cancer. Agent Orange was a defoliant sprayed on jungles in Vietnam to rid the Viet Cong of their hiding places. Many Army and Marine combat troops were exposed to it, but I had been a helicopter mechanic working at a secure air base, not fighting in the jungles. How did I come in contact with Agent Orange? It was determined by the VA that my working on helicopters which had been in contact with Agent Orange is what did me in. And that's how my cancer began – similar to getting cancer from second-hand smoke from a cigarette.

A couple years ago, I wrote my first booklet about my journey with cancer. It is titled *Prepared to Die but Totally Unprepared to Live*, and it is still available on Amazon Books. God, so far, has given me four extra years to live since my cancer was discovered back in 2018, but my life has been drastically changed.

Life goes on. I'm now looking ahead more and more and looking back less and less. God has been good to me.

CPSIA information can be obtained
at www.ICGtesting.com
Printed in the USA
LVHW040909020423
743259LV00003B/108